Marvin's Shining Star

Story by John Otto and Payton Otto

Illustrations by Janelda Lane

THE ROADRUNNER PRESS
OKLAHOMA CITY, OKLAHOMA

Published by The RoadRunner Press

Catalog-in-Publication Data is on file at OCLC and SkyRiver and viewable at www.WorldCat.org

ISBN: 978-1-937054-77-9
Library of Congress Control Number: 2014954741
Printed in October 2014 in the United States of America

First Edition
10 9 8 7 6 5 4 3 2 1

For the children of the incarcerated and Sister Pauline,

whose vision began the prison dog programs

Marvin was born on an Oklahoma farm with a pond. He had two brothers and a sister, and he liked helping with the farm animals. He scattered corn for the chickens. He shoveled slop for the pigs.

As he grew older, Marvin grew as tall as a cornstalk and as broad as a barn. His love for the animals on the farm grew too, especially for the dogs.

Then one day Marvin decided he was so big
he did not need to listen to his parents anymore.
He began to get into trouble with his brothers at
school. He got into more trouble outside of school.

Marvin started to lie . . . sometimes to protect his
brothers, like the time Tyrone broke a window. Marvin
said he broke the window. One lie led to another. One
bad deed led to the next. And then one day, Marvin

and Tyrone did something terrible to someone.
One more time, Marvin told a lie to protect his
brother. Only this time he lied to the police,
and the police put Marvin and Tyrone in jail.

Marvin was sad about what he had done, and he missed his home on the farm. He missed his animals. He missed his dogs most of all. He felt all alone.

Every night Marvin dreamed of being back on the farm with his sister and brothers. In his dreams, Marvin always took time to play fetch with his dogs.

Many years passed. Marvin had now lived in prison more years than he had lived on the farm. Every day was the same. He wondered if it would always be like that.

Then one day the warden made an announcement: the very best inmates—those who never lost their temper, who did what they were asked to do, and who worked and studied hard—would be allowed to train rescue dogs in the Friends for Folks program.

Suddenly, Marvin had hope. Marvin worked hard. Marvin studied hard. Marvin refused to fight when others teased him. More than anything in the world, Marvin wanted to be picked to train the rescue dogs.

And so he was.

The rescue dogs came from the red dirt roads and the city streets of Oklahoma. They came from families who did not take care of them. They came from families who had let them run wild.

All the rescue dogs had problems, but now they had someone to help turn them into the dogs they were meant to be.

The dogs lived with the inmates in their cells. Two big dogs plus two big men made for very tight quarters, but Marvin never complained. Having a dog again was a little like being home, and since the dogs had arrived, there were fewer fights in the prison yard.

One day Marvin met a veterinarian named Dr. John Otto. Dr. Otto came to give the dogs their vaccinations and to make sure they were fed and brushed every day. Dr. Otto noticed how kind Marvin was to all the dogs, and Dr. Otto and Marvin became friends.

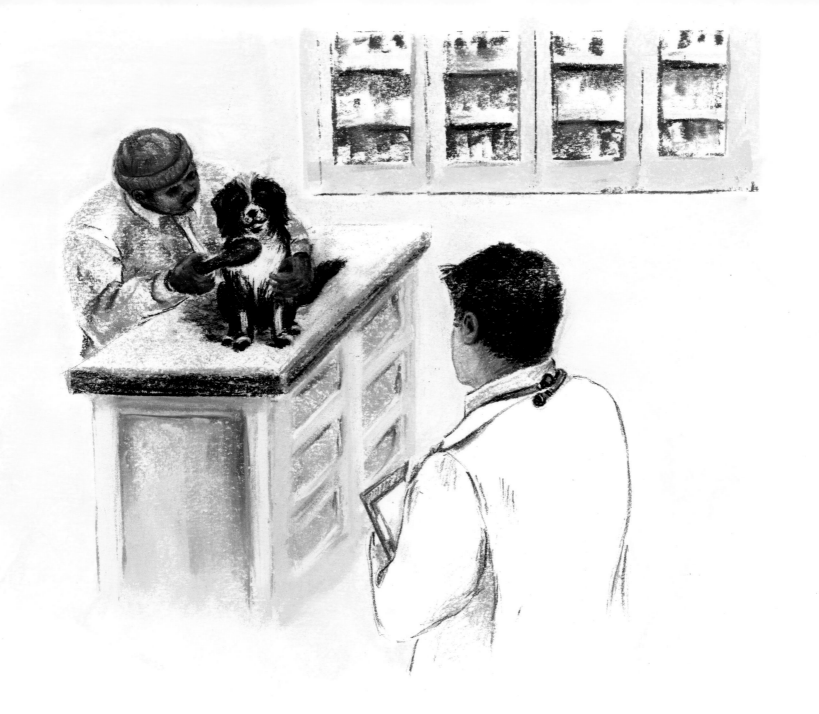

Marvin helped build a kennel for the dogs. The dogs liked it so much Marvin helped build a pond for them, like the one on Marvin's old family farm. It was hard work, but working hard made Marvin feel better.

That very well could have been that, except one day a prison guard named Tracy found a puppy at the Norman Animal Shelter and decided to rescue it. The puppy was black with a little white star on her chest.

Tracy brought the puppy to Marvin to be trained, and the puppy ran right into Marvin's arms. Marvin named the puppy Star for the white mark on her coat.

Marvin and Star were together all the time. They slept together. They trained together. And they played together. Star's favorite game was hide-and-seek. No matter where Marvin hid, Star could find him.

Marvin told Dr. Otto he thought Star was meant to be a search-and-rescue dog. Dr. Otto agreed.

Marvin and Star trained every day. Soon Star was the best search-and-rescue dog at the prison.

One evening an elderly woman went missing in a
nearby town. No one could find her—not the police in
their helicopters, not the best police search dogs, not the
search teams on foot. Everyone was about to give up
when Tracy, the prison guard, remembered Marvin's Star.

Tracy asked if Star could come help look for the woman.

Marvin gave Star a pep talk. "Go find her, girl," he said.

And sure enough, what the others couldn't do in hours,

Star did in less than twenty minutes in the dark: she

found the missing woman trapped in a steep ravine.

Soon everyone had heard about what Star had done. Dr. Otto wrote a letter nominating Star for the Pet Hall of Fame Hero Award, and out of all the brave and good dogs nominated, the Oklahoma Veterinary Medical Association gave the gold medal to Star.

Star was a hero! Marvin was so proud.

Dr. Otto knew Marvin had worked long and hard to atone for his mistakes. Marvin had become the man he was meant to be. Dr. Otto decided to write another letter. This time he wrote the Governor of Oklahoma about Marvin and the good Marvin had done. Dr. Otto asked if Marvin could be given a second chance.

Governor Brad Henry said, "Yes!"

Once he was free, Marvin often dropped by to see
Dr. Otto and his son, Payton, on the Otto farm.
Fixing fences or sipping lemonade with the Ottos
recalled the happiest days of his childhood.

Marvin got a job taking care of a big hotel in the city
and a little place of his own. He liked nothing better
than having family dinners with his daughter, Marva,
who had grown up while he was gone.

Star moved to Tracy's house so she could
keep finding more missing people.

Thanks to Marvin and Star, Friends for Folks is in more
correctional facilties than ever before, helping men and
women atone for their mistakes. The men and women
train dogs for search-and-rescue teams and to be
companions for the elderly and others
who might have need of a furry friend.

As for Dr. Otto, whenever he sees the first star in the night
sky, he always says a little prayer for his friend Marvin,
and then he makes a wish . . .

. . . that all the Stars in the world might get a second chance, just like Marvin's Shining Star.

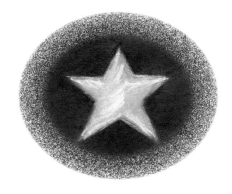

The End

About Marvin, Star,
and Friends for Folks

Sister Pauline Quinn started the first prison dog program in Washington State in 1981.
The program is now in thirty-four states and several countries.

In 1990, veterinarian Grant Turnwald and others started Friends for Folks
at Lexington Correctional Center in Lexington, Oklahoma.
It is one of the oldest prison dog programs in the United States.

Veterinarian John Otto, the son of a former acting director of the FBI,
began volunteering with Friends for Folks in 1996. More than 1,000 rescue
and shelter dogs have been saved through the program.

In 2012, Greg Mellott of Oklahoma City Community College's Film and Video
Program and six of his students made a documentary about the Lexington prison dog program.
The Dogs of Lexington aired in 2013 and was a finalist for an Emmy Award.

In 2014, Dr. Otto introduced the Friends for Folks program to Mabel Bassett
Correctional Center, a facility for female offenders outside McCloud, Oklahoma.
Film director Greg Mellott's new documentary, *Bassett Tales*, about how the
Friends for Folks program came to Mabel Bassett will air at the end of 2014.

Marvin Perry was paroled in 2007 by Oklahoma Governor Brad Henry
after being recognized for the discipline, compassion, and training he had
exhibited in turning Star into a valued search-and-rescue dog.

Star is now retired and lives with one of the program's original trainers.
Marvin died of Lou Gehrig's disease in July 2012.

In loving memory of Marvin